P9-AEU-349

The Teachers' Book of Wisdom

A Celebration of the Joys of Teaching

Dr. Criswell Freeman

WG
WALNUT GROVE PRESS
NASHVILLE, TN

T The eachers'
Book of Wisdom

A Celebration of the Joys of Teaching

Dr. Criswell Freeman

©2002 Walnut Grove Press

All rights reserved. Except for brief quotations used in reviews, articles, or other media, no part of this book may be reproduced or transmitted in any form or by any means, electronic or mechanical, including photocopy, recording or by information storage or retrieval system, without permission by the publisher.

Walnut Grove Press
Nashville, TN 37203

2nd Edition
ISBN 1-58334-139-0

The ideas expressed in this book are not, in all cases, exact quotations, as some have been edited for clarity and brevity. In all cases, the author has attempted to maintain the speaker's original intent. In some cases, material for this book was obtained from secondary sources, primarily print media. While every effort was made to ensure the accuracy of these sources, the accuracy cannot be guaranteed. For additions, deletions, corrections or clarifications in future editions of this text, please write Walnut Grove Press.

Printed in the United States of America
Cover & Page Layout Design by Bart Dawson
Cover Photo: www.comstock.com
1 2 3 4 5 6 7 8 9 10 • 02 03 04 05 06 07 08 09 10

Acknowledgments: The author is indebted to Angela Freeman, Dick and Mary Freeman, Ron Smith, Jim Gallery, and to the creative staff at Walnut Grove Press.

For Donna

The Table of Contents

Introduction

Teachers touch the lives of their students on countless occasions. Each time a single life is touched, even in some small way, eternity is refashioned.

Savvy teachers create a classroom environment that is conducive to learning. Then, they make the subject interesting. And finally, they hold their students accountable for the work that must be done. Teachers challenge their students and may even change the ways in which their students look at the world. And, teachers can provide essential tools for life beyond the classroom. What profession is more important than this?

The quotations in this book celebrate the joys of teaching. May we all celebrate the talents and accomplishments of those who help shape the minds of the next generation, and may we all continue to teach—and learn—forever.

1

The Joy of Teaching

A teacher affects
eternity; he can
never tell where
his influence stops.

—*Henry Adams*—

Molding the minds of young people is a profound responsibility and, at times, a royal headache. Sometimes teachers are overburdened with too much work and too little time in which to do it. Sometimes students misbehave. Sometimes parents are unreasonable. And sometimes, there are too few dollars in the school's budget and too many students in the teacher's classroom. But, despite the inevitable nuisances of grading, preparation, paperwork and classroom discipline, teaching is, at its best, a joyful profession.

In this chapter, we consider the delights and responsibilities of the teacher's life. May the delights always outweigh the headaches.

Teaching means helping the child
realize his potential.

Erich Fromm

People who never get carried away should be.

Malcolm Forbes

Every production of genius must be
the production of enthusiasm.

Benjamin Disraeli

It is enough that I am of value
to somebody today.

Hugh Prather

What could be more important than equipping
the next generation with the character and
competence they need to become successful?

Colin Powell

My heart is singing for joy this morning.
A miracle has happened! The light of
understanding has shone upon my little pupil's
mind, and, behold, all things are changed!

Annie Sullivan

Teachers not only create a desire for thought,
they give a student experience in thinking.

John Sloan Dickey

"You are happy," the true ethics whisper.
"Therefore you are called upon to give much."

Albert Schweitzer

What office is there which involves more
responsibility, which requires more
qualifications, and which ought, therefore,
to be more honorable than that of teaching?

Harriet Martineau

If you want to be successful, it's just this simple:
Know what you're doing.
Love what you're doing.
And believe in what you're doing.

Will Rogers

The truth is that I am enslaved…
in one vast love affair with 70 children.

Sylvia Ashton-Warner

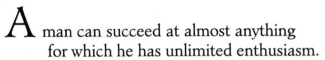
A man can succeed at almost anything
    for which he has unlimited enthusiasm.

Charles M. Schwab

Man never rises to great truths
      without enthusiasm.

Vauvenargues

Knowledge is power, but enthusiasm
      pulls the switch.

Ivern Ball

When enthusiasm is inspired by reason;
    controlled by caution; sound in theory;
practical in application; reflects confidence;
spreads good cheer; raises morale; inspires
    associates; arouses loyalty; and
laughs at adversity, it is beyond price.

Coleman Cox

I'm never going to be a movie star. But then, in all probability, Liz Taylor is never going to teach first and second grade.

Mary J. Wilson

Zeal will do more than knowledge.

William Hazlitt

Child, give me your hand that I may walk in the light of your faith in me.

Hannah Kahn

All my pupils are the crème de la crème. Give me a girl of an impressionable age, and she is mine for life.

Muriel Spark

The Courage to Dream

Walt Disney once observed, "All our dreams can come true if we only have the courage to pursue them." But sometimes our children are afraid to dream big dreams because they fear failure. Wise teachers know that there are far worse things in this world than failure (like failing to try, for example), so they encourage their students to aim high, to work hard, to follow through, and to expect success. Then, armed with confidence and competence, students can do great things because they have the courage to dream...and the faith to believe that their dreams can come true.

A teacher makes
two ideas
where only one
grew before.

—Elbert Hubbard—

2

Education Is...

Education is
not merely a means
for earning a living or
an instrument for the
acquisition of wealth.
It is an initiation into a
life of spirit, a training
of the human soul in
the pursuit of truth and
the practice of virtue.

—Vijaya Lakshmi Pandit—

What is education? Education defies simple definition because it occurs in so many different locations and on so many different levels. Of course education takes place inside the classroom, but it also takes place in countless other settings. We learn from books, teachers, parents, coaches, bosses, and peers. Sometimes, wisdom comes from observation, other times only from bitter experience.

Perhaps the best definition of education was proposed by American philanthropist George Peabody. He said, "Education is a debt from present to future generations." In this chapter, we consider the implications of that debt along with intelligent plans for repayment.

Education is a chest of tools.

Herbert Kaufman

There are two educations.
One should teach us how to make a living
and the other how to live.

James Truslow Adams

Education is hanging on until you've caught on.

Robert Frost

Training is everything. The peach was once
a bitter almond; cauliflower is nothing
but cabbage with a college education.

Mark Twain

The acquisition of knowledge is the mission
of research; the transmission of
knowledge is the mission of teaching;
and the application of knowledge
is the mission of public service.

James A. Perkins

Education is a better safeguard of liberty
than a standing army.

Edward Everett

Without education, what is man?
A splendid slave, a reasoning savage.

Joseph Addison

Education is training for duty.

Berthold Auerbach

Education, beyond all other devices of
human origin, is the great equalizer
of the conditions of men—the balance-wheel
of the social machinery.

Horace Mann

We must see that every child has equal
opportunity, not to become equal, but
to become different—to realize
the unique potential he or she possesses.

John Fischer

Education is that which leads one
to the right loves and hatreds.

Lin Yutang

The object of education is to get experience
out of ideas.

George Santayana

The purpose of education is to awaken joy
in creative expression and knowledge.

Albert Einstein

Perhaps the most valuable results of all education
is the ability to make yourself do
the thing you have to do, when it ought
to be done, whether you like it or not.
It is the first lesson that ought to be learned.

Thomas Huxley

Education takes place in the combination
of the home, the community,
the school, and the receptive mind.

Harry Edwards

Education means capacity for further education.

John Dewey

Sixty years ago, I knew everything;
now I know nothing; education is
a progressive discovery
of our own ignorance.

Will Durant

A degree is not an education, and the
confusion on this point is perhaps
the gravest weakness in education.

Rockefeller Brothers Fund

When the pupil is ready, the teacher will come.

Chinese Saying

Much that passes for education is not
education at all, but ritual. The fact is that
we are being educated when we know it least.

David P. Gardner

An education isn't how much you have
committed to memory. It's knowing where to
go to find out what you need to know, and it's
knowing how to use the information you get.

William Feather

Knowledge is not simply another commodity.
To the contrary, knowledge is never used up.
It increases by diffusion and
grows by dispersion.

Daniel J. Boorstin

Education is a kind of continuing dialogue,
and a dialogue assumes different
points of view.

Robert M. Hutchins

Education is a matter of building bridges.

Ralph Ellison

Education should convert the mind into
a living fountain and not a reservoir.

John M. Mason

The ability to think straight, some knowledge
of the past, some vision of the future, some skill
to do useful service, some urge to fit that
service into the well-being of the community—
these are the most vital things education
must try to produce.

Virginia Gildersleeve

Real education should educate us out of self
into something far finer—into selflessness
which links us with all humanity.

Nancy Astor

Prejudice is the child of ignorance.

William Hazlitt

The basic purpose of a liberal arts education
is to liberate the human being to exercise
his or her potential to the fullest.

Barbara M. White

There are few earthly things more beautiful
than a university.

John Masefield

Universities should be safe havens where
ruthless examination of realities will not be
distorted by the aim to please or inhibited
by the risk of displeasure.

Kingman Brewster

A university's essential character is that of
being a center of free inquiry and
criticism—a thing not to be sacrificed
for anything else.

Richard Hofstadter

College is a refuge from hasty judgment.

Robert Frost

The most important thing about education
is appetite.

Winston Churchill

The teacher's task is not to implant facts but
to place the subject to be learned in front
of the learner and, through sympathy,
emotion, imagination and patience,
to awaken in the learner the restless drive
for answers and insights which enlarge
the personal life and give it meaning.

Nathan M. Pusey

Via ovicipitum dura est.
(The way of the egghead is hard.)

Adlai E. Stevenson

Education is the seeing of things
in the working.

Thomas Alva Edison

Education is the ability to listen to almost
anything without losing your temper
or your self-confidence.

Robert Frost

Only the educated are free.

Epictetus

Learning "The Basics"

The old familiar song praises the value of "readin' and writin' and 'rithmetic." And it still applies. Every child deserves an early exposure to the joys of reading, and every student deserves an education in the basics of grammar and mathematics. When we allow our children to pass through the halls of academia without a firm grasp of the fundamental tools of learning, we do them a profound disservice—one with lifelong ramifications. But, when we prepare our youth with a firm foundation grounded in the basics of reading, writing, and mathematics, we prepare them for success, and we help provide for generations that are yet unborn.

The only thing more expensive than education is ignorance.

—Ben Franklin—

3

The Power
of Education

Better to have education than wealth.

—Welsh Proverb—

Francis Bacon wrote, "Knowledge and human power are synonymous." His words are truer today than ever. By and large, the uneducated must play the entire game of life on an uneven field. But, the value of education is often invisible to young people who rebel against the very tool that might level the field on which they play—or even tilt that field in their direction.

Fairness and common sense dictate that every boy and girl be given a meaningful opportunity to learn; the rest, of course, is out of teachers' hands. Only parents and students possess the ability to harness the power of education, but good teachers can show them how.

The education of a man is never completed
until he dies.

Robert E. Lee

The test and the use of man's education
is that he finds pleasure in the exercise
of his mind.

Jacques Barzun

Learning makes a man fit company
for himself.

Thomas Fuller

If we work upon marble, it will perish; if we
work on brass, time will efface it. If we rear
temples, they will crumble to dust. But if we work
on men's immortal minds, if we impress on them
high principles, the just fear of God, and love for
their fellowmen, we engrave on those tablets
something which no time can efface and
which will brighten and brighten to all eternity.

Daniel Webster

The aim of education is the knowledge
not of facts but of values.

William Ralph Inge

He knows enough who knows how to learn.

Henry Adams

Think wrongly, if you please, but in all cases,
think for yourself.

Doris Lessing

The efficient man is the man who thinks
for himself.

Charles W. Eliot

Curiosity is the one permanent and
certain characteristic of a vigorous mind.

Samuel Johnson

The human mind is our fundamental resource.

John F. Kennedy

In the realm of ideas, it is better to let the
mind sally forth, even if some precious
preconceptions suffer a mauling.

Robert F. Goheen

Any education that matters is liberal.
All the saving truths, all the healing graces
that distinguish a good education from a bad one
or a full education from a half empty one are
contained in that word.

Alan Simpson

An educated man is one who can entertain
a new idea, entertain another person,
and entertain himself.

Sydney Wood

The mind's cross-indexing puts the best
librarian to shame.

Sharon Begley

The important thing is to not stop questioning.

Albert Einstein

I know no safe depository of the ultimate
powers of the society but the people themselves;
and if we think them not enlightened enough
to exercise their control with a wholesome
discretion, the remedy is not to take it from
them but to inform their discretion by
education. This is the true corrective
of abuses of constitutional power.

Thomas Jefferson

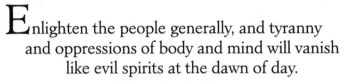

Enlighten the people generally, and tyranny
and oppressions of body and mind will vanish
like evil spirits at the dawn of day.

Thomas Jefferson

Genius means little more than the faculty
of perceiving in an unhabitual way.

William James

Whether you think you can or think you can't,
you're right.

Henry Ford

It is safer to have a whole people respectably
enlightened than a few in a high state
of science and the many in ignorance.

Thomas Jefferson

The benefits of education and of useful knowledge, generally diffused through a community, are essential to the preservation of a free government.

Sam Houston

The direction of the mind is more important than its progress.

Joseph Joubert

Nothing can possibly afford greater stability to a popular government than the education of its people.

Samuel Whitbread

Education is the foundation of governance.

Jacob H. Carruthers

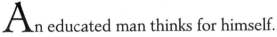

An educated man thinks for himself.

Alan Simpson

Human history becomes more and more
a race between education and catastrophe.

H. G. Wells

Upon the education of the people of this
country the fate of this country depends.

Benjamin Disraeli

In the long course of history, having an educated
electorate is much greater security
than another submarine.

J. William Fulbright

Just as those who have to live upon coarse
food may show its effects in their body,
so those whose minds are fed upon pure thought,
whether of Longfellow or Whittier or
any other first-class poet, will soon show
in their spiritual development what
they have been studying.

Fanny Jackson Coppin

To educate a man in mind and not in morals
is to educate a menace to society.

Theodore Roosevelt

If you drop out, you miss out.

Bill Cosby

Education has for its object the formation
of character. This is the aim of both
parent and teacher.

Herbert Spencer

The Value of Education

Teachers understand the value of education. Students often do not. Thus the first lesson that a good teacher must often teach is the importance of a solid, well-rounded education.

Education is the tool by which we come to know and appreciate the world in which we live. It is the shining light that snuffs out the darkness of ignorance and poverty. Education is freedom just as surely as ignorance is a form of bondage. Education is not a luxury, it is a necessity and a powerful tool for good. Let us teach our children to value it always.

Give a man a fish and
you feed him for a day.
Teach a man to fish
and you feed him
for a lifetime.

—Chinese Proverb—

4

The Learning
Experience

Learning is the discovery that something is possible.

—Fritz Perls—

Aristotle observed, "All men by nature desire to learn." It might be added that some men seem to desire it more than others. And what makes the difference? In part, the difference is superior teaching. Outstanding teachers do much more than convey knowledge; they also spur the desire to learn.

British mathematician Alfred North Whitehead wrote, "From the very beginning of his education, the child should experience the joy of discovery." The learning experience is, at its best, a grand adventure with teachers serving as tour guides. The following ideas will help in planning the tour.

Only the curious will learn, and only the
resolute will overcome the obstacles to learning.
The quest quotient has always excited me
more than the intelligence quotient.

Eugene S. Wilson

Learning is a natural pleasure, inborn and
instinctive, one of the earliest pleasures
and one of the essential pleasures
of the human race.

Gilbert Highet

It is what we think we know already that
prevents us from learning.

Claude Bernard

To live for a time close to great minds
is the best kind of education.

John Buchan

We learn simply by the exposure of living,
and what we learn most natively
is the tradition in which we live.

David P. Gardner

Too often, for many of us, learning appears
to be an imposition, a surrender of our own
willpower to external direction, indeed a sort
of enslavement. This is a mistake.

Gilbert Highet

That is what learning is. You suddenly understand
something you've understood all your life,
but in a new way.

Doris Lessing

Learning means
keeping the mind open
and active to receive
all kinds of experience.

—Gilbert Highet—

The process of learning can and must become
not only one of growing but also of sharing.

Joe Nathan

In a time of drastic change, it is the learners
who inherit the future.

Eric Hoffer

All learning proceeds by steps. Absences of
pupils are like a ladder with a rung out here
and there. Instead of going up easily,
the student every now and then is distracted
by the difficulty of the step.

Fanny Jackson Coppin

Learning is more difficult for the young
if it is a "have-to" imposed by authority.

Gilbert Highet

All our children deserve teachers
who believe they can learn and who
will not be satisfied until they do.

Joe Nathan

The days in my life that stand out most vividly
are the days I've learned something.
Learning is so exciting that
I get goose bumps.

Lucille Ball

Even if we live for ninety years, we can never
exhaust the pleasures
of poetry or art or music.

Gilbert Highet

I was still learning when I taught my last class.

Claude M. Fuess

Most of the important experiences
that truly educate cannot be arranged
ahead of time with any precision.

Harold Taylor

Schoolmasters and parents exist
to be grown out of.

John Wolfenden

Four years was enough of Harvard. I still had
a lot to learn but had been given the liberating
notion that now I could teach myself.

John Updike

Could *Hamlet* have been written by a
committee, or the Mona Lisa painted by a club?
Could the New Testament have been composed
as a conference report? Creative ideas do not
spring from groups. They spring from individuals.
The divine spark leaps from the finger
of God to the finger of Adam.

A. Whitney Griswold

If they are willing to learn, the quality
of their lives will improve.

William Glasser, M.D.

The function of education is to teach one to
think intensively and to think critically.
Intelligence plus character—that is
the goal of true education.

Martin Luther King, Jr.

What a teacher doesn't say is a telling part
of what a student hears.

Maurice Natanson

Lifetime Learning

Teachers understand the importance of lifetime learning, but students may not see the value of continuing edcation. After all, students often tire of textbooks, tests, classrooms, and computer screens. Still, as every teacher knows, formal schooling should constitute the beginning, not the end, of a student's education.

Once the sheepskin is safely signed and framed, graduates are free to concentrate on their own studies. When they do, they claim the lifelong rewards that result from a liberal education: the infinite possibilities and opportunities that are available to those wise men and women who keep learning every day that they live.

No one ever became wise by chance.

—Seneca—

5

Books

There is more treasure
in books than in
all the pirate's loot
on Treasure Island.

—Walt Disney—

Noted psychologist B. F. Skinner observed, "We shouldn't teach great books; we should teach a love of reading." The ability to enjoy a good book is an acquired skill that pays lifelong dividends. The following quotations celebrate the joy of reading. And now, with no further ado, let the celebration begin!

To acquire the habit of reading is to construct
for yourself a refuge from almost all
the miseries of life.

Somerset Maugham

Books are friends that never fail.

Thomas Carlyle

No matter how busy you may think you are,
you must find time for reading, or surrender
yourself to self-chosen ignorance.

Atwood H. Townsend

The very concept of history implies the
scholar and the reader. Without a generation
of civilized people to study history, to preserve
its records, to absorb its lessons and relate
them to its own problems, history, too,
would lose its meaning.

George F. Kennan

Books are a guide in youth
and an entertainment in old age.

Jeremy Collier

Books are the very heart and core of ages past.

Amy Lowell

A good book is opened with expectation
and closed with profit.

Bronson Alcott

The elementary school must assume as its
sublime and most solemn responsibility
the task of teaching every child in it to read.
Any school that does not accomplish
this has failed.

Jacques Barzun

A book is a garden carried in the pocket.

Arabian Proverb

Books are not made for furniture,
but there is nothing else that
so beautifully furnishes a house.

Henry Ward Beecher

Happy are the children whose parents know
the importance of teaching them to love
and care for books while they
are young.

Fanny Jackson Coppin

Books are the windows through which
the souls look out.

Henry Ward Beecher

Books are the true university.

Thomas Carlyle

A good library is a joyful place
where the imagination roams free,
and life is actively enriched.

John K. Hutchens

A library, to modify the famous metaphor
of Socrates, should be the delivery room
for the birth of ideas—a place
where history comes to life.

Norman Cousins

Libraries keep the records
on behalf of all humanity.

Vartan Gregorian

Reading books contains two different delights,
both definable as learning. One is the pleasure
of apprehending the unexpected: when one meets
a new author who has a new vision of the world.
The other is the pleasure of deepening one's
knowledge of a special field.

Gilbert Highet

Sometimes when I stand in a big library,
I feel a sober, earnest delight which is hard to
convey. These are not books, lumps of lifeless
paper, but *minds* alive on the shelves.

Gilbert Highet

A book is one of the few places left where
a man's mind can get both
provocation and privacy.

Edward P. Morgan

What is important—what lasts—in another
language is not what is said but what is written.
For the essence of an age, we look to its poetry
and its prose, not its talk shows.

Peter Brodie

The Value of a Book

What is the value of a good book? It depends. Books that enlighten us, or encourage us, or entertain us, or educate us have the potential for great value. But, books that are left unread on the shelf are nothing more than decorations.

When a good book falls into the hands of an enthusiastic reader, a spark is ignited that can burn from the first page to the last. Our challenge, as teachers, is to introduce good students to good books and hope that the resulting flames will burn for a lifetime.

Books are the fit inheritance of generations and nations.

—Henry David Thoreau—

6

The Art of Teaching

Teaching is
the art of
assisting discovery.

—Mark Van Doren—

Exceptional teachers come in many shapes and sizes, but they all share a few essential traits. The best instructors not only challenge their students but also encourage them. Outstanding teachers also entertain while they educate. Finally, exceptional teachers understand that the most important lesson—and the teacher's greatest challenge—is to instill the love of learning in the heart of the pupil.

Great educators, like great artists, create works that outlive their creators. Teachers leave their mark on a human canvas. In this chapter, we consider ways to improve the artwork.

A teacher who is attempting to teach
without inspiring the pupil with a desire
to learn is hammering on cold iron.

Horace Mann

What is really important in education is not
that the child learn this and that, but that
the mind is matured and energy is aroused.

Søren Kierkegaard

Teaching is not the filling of the pail
but the lighting of the fire.

William Butler Yeats

To know how to suggest is
the great art of teaching.

Ralph Waldo Emerson

Better than a thousand days of diligent study
is one day with a great teacher.

Japanese Proverb

A great teacher makes hard things easy.

Ralph Waldo Emerson

A good teacher, like a good entertainer,
first must hold his audience's attention.
Then he can teach the lesson.

John Henrik Clarke

The greatest artist is the simplifier.

Henri Frédéric Amiel

A teacher is one who brings us tools
and enables us to use them.

Jean Toomer

Teaching is an instinctual art, mindful of
potential, craving of realization,
a pausing, seamless process.

A. Bartlett Giamatti

Teachers are the unsung heroes of society.

Christine Modisher

Teaching is not a lost art, but
the regard for it is a lost tradition.

Jacques Barzun

Human beings are full of emotion,
and the teacher who knows how to use it
will have dedicated learners.

Leon Lessinger

Teachers believe they have a gift for giving;
it drives them with the same irrepressible drive
that drives others to create a work of art or
a market or a building.

A. Bartlett Giamatti

The art of teaching is the art of awakening
the natural curiosity of young minds.

Anatole France

On a good day, I view the job as directing
an orchestra. On the dark days, it is more like
that of a clutch—engaging the engine
to effect forward motion.

A. Bartlett Giamatti

A teacher must believe in the value and
interest of his subject as
a doctor believes in health.

Gilbert Highet

Effective teaching will not always be
entertaining, but it will engage youngsters
in thoughtful, productive activity.

Joe Nathan

I have one rule—attention.
They give me theirs, and I give them mine.

Sister Evangelist RSM

The good teacher discovers the natural gifts
of his pupils and liberates them by the
stimulating influence of the inspiration that
he can impart. The true leader makes
his followers twice the men they were before.

Stephen Neill

Everyone knows a good deal
about one child—himself.

Dora Chaplin

The only gift is a portion of thyself.

Ralph Waldo Emerson

In the washroom, we need a soap dispenser.
In the classroom, we need a hope dispenser.

Marie T. Freeman

The only reason I always try to meet and
know the parents better is because it
helps me to forgive their children.

Louis Johannot

A substantial body of research supports
the common-sense notion that young people
do not learn as much in a threatening
environment as in a supportive one.

Joe Nathan

Who dares to teach must never cease to learn.

John Cotton Dana

Above all, leave room for your own learning—
for the chance to discover and teach something
you didn't know when the course began.

Wayne C. Booth

Teaching demands not just desirable personality
attributes but specific skills. Skills are not ends
in themselves, but they are necessary tools.

Jacob S. Kounin

Many a child called dull would advance
rapidly under a patient, wise and skillful teacher,
and the teacher should be as conscientious in
the endeavor to improve himself as he
is to improve the child.

Fanny Jackson Coppin

Men learn while they teach.

Seneca

All teachers know enough to know that only useful work can provide the incentive students need to expend the effort to do quality work.

William Glasser, M.D.

Every class should be for you as much as for the students.

Wayne C. Booth

As you teach, emphasize what interests you.

William Glasser, M.D.

If we think about our own lives, we'll remember how much more we learned from those who encouraged us.

Joe Nathan

The essence of teaching is to make
learning contagious,
to have one idea spark another.

Marva Collins

Teachers must think for themselves if they
are to help others think for themselves.

Carnegie Corporation of New York

I had learned to respect the intelligence,
integrity, creativity and capacity for
deep thought and hard work latent
somewhere in every child.

Sybil Marshall

The Art of Encouragement

Learning the skill of encouragement is part of the art of teaching. And make no mistake: encouragement is a skill that is learned over time and improved with constant use. How, we ask, can we be most encouraging? The answer is found, in part, by reminding ourselves what genuine encouragement is and what it is not.

The dictionary defines encouragement as, "the act of inspiring courage and confidence." Genuine encouragement is not idle flattery nor is it pity. It is instead the transfer of courage from one person to another. It is a firm reminder of the teacher's confidence in the student's talents, strengths, resources and opportunities. When that confidence is internalized by the student, miracles can happen.

Words, words, how they can make or mar our lives!

—Fanny Jackson Coppin—

7

The Student

A child miseducated is a child lost.

—John F. Kennedy—

Educator Fanny Jackson Coppin noted, "I'm always sorry to hear that a person is going to school to be educated. This is a great mistake. If a person is to get the benefit of what we call education, he must educate himself, under the direction of the teacher." In other words, you can lead a boy to wonder, but you can't make him think.

The following quotations give insight into the hearts and minds of those who, in the end, must educate themselves. And when they do, what a glorious sight to behold!

Happy is the child who has wise parents
and guardians and whose training is
continued when he enters the school room.

Fanny Jackson Coppin

I see the mind of the 5-year-old
as a volcano with two vents:
destructiveness and creativeness.

Sylvia Ashton-Warner

The teacher can lead a student to the door;
the acquisition of learning is the
responsibility of the student.

Chinese Proverb

All students can learn.

Christopher Morley

Most of the trouble and friction among people,
in or out of school, is caused
by putting others down.

William Glasser, M.D.

Native ability without education
is like a tree without fruit.

Aristippus

Start a program for gifted children, and every
parent demands that his child be enrolled.

Thomas Bailey

There must be such a thing as a child with
average ability, but you can't find a parent
who will admit that it is his child.

Thomas Bailey

A student is not a professional athlete.
He is not a little politician or junior senator
looking for angles. A student is a person who is
learning to fulfill his powers and to find ways
of using them in the service of mankind.

Harold Taylor

Anyone who's watched a school's doors
at the end of the day knows how much
human energy bursts out at the final bell.
The potential is there, waiting to be stimulated,
challenged, and encouraged.

Joe Nathan

If you promise not to believe everything your
child says happens at this school,
I'll promise not to believe everything he
says happens at home.

Anonymous

We cannot learn from one another until
we stop shouting at one another, until
we speak quietly enough so that our words
can be heard as well as our voices.

Richard M. Nixon

Work 'em hard, play 'em hard, feed 'em up to
the nines and send 'em to bed so tired that
they are asleep before their heads
are on the pillow.

Frank L. Boyden

Students welcome any change from routine.

William Glasser, M.D.

In the conditions of modern life, the rule
is absolute: Those who do not value trained
intelligence are doomed. There is no appeal
from the judgment which is pronounced
on the uneducated.

Alfred North Whitehead

Let early education be a sort of amusement;
you will then be better able to discover
the child's natural bent.

Plato

If you plan for a year, plant a seed. If for
ten years, plant a tree. If for a hundred years,
teach the people. When you sow a seed once,
you will reap a single harvest. When you teach
the people, you will reap a hundred harvests.

Kuan Chung

The quality of a university is measured more
by the kind of student it turns out
than the kind it takes in.

Robert J. Kibbee

Lessons in Self-worth

Comedienne Lucille Ball was once asked to share the best advice she had learned over a long and eventful life. Lucy responded simply, "Love yourself first." Teachers everywhere understand that message.

All too often, students enter the classroom with lowered self-esteem; in such cases, thoughtful teachers seek to infuse those students with a heightened sense of self-worth. Lessons in self-esteem are seldom found in textbooks, but such lessons are, in some cases, more important than the assigned schoolwork.

Teachers understand that all students have value (even when the students themselves believe otherwise). Teachers who share a message of encouragement and self-acceptance give their students a gift that can last a lifetime.

Our young people
need to know we have
discovered the seeds of
greatness within them.

—Anonymous—

$$\overline{}$$

8

Homework

Well done is better than well said.

—Ben Franklin—

When times get tough in the old schoolhouse, most students react in a similar fashion: They blame the teacher. This blame is almost always misdirected. Pupils are advised to contemplate the words of Shakespeare's Cassius, who admitted, "The fault, dear Brutus, is not in our stars, but in ourselves...."

Socrates observed, "If a man would move the world, he must first move himself." And so it is with education. The student who wishes to move to the head of the class must begin by moving himself in that direction. While the teacher may help show the way, the student himself makes the journey. If the results of that journey are unsatisfactory, it profits no one to accuse instructors, institutions, or the heavens. Any pupil who feels the urge to blame a teacher should try a more constructive strategy: doing the homework.

The day is short, the labor long,
the workers are idle, the reward is great,
and the Master is urgent.

Rabbi Tarfon

Being ignorant is not so much a shame
as being unwilling to learn.

Ben Franklin

The main value of homework lies in the
experience it gives a child
to work on his own.

Haim Ginott

When you have a number of disagreeable
duties to perform, always do the most
disagreeable first.

Josiah Quincy

The world belongs to the energetic.

Ralph Waldo Emerson

Fear is nature's warning sign to get busy.

Henry C. Link

I do not know anyone who has got to the top
without hard work. That's the recipe.
It will not always get you to the top
but should get you pretty near.

Margaret Thatcher

The reward of a thing well done
is to have done it.

Ralph Waldo Emerson

Perseverance can do anything
which genius can do and
very many things which genius cannot.

Henry Ward Beecher

It is not labor that kills but the small
attritions of daily routine
that wear us down.

Roy Bedicheck

Our greatest weariness comes
from work not done.

Eric Hoffer

The willingness to accept responsibility
for one's own life is the source from
which self-respect springs.

Joan Didion

The world is blessed most by men who do things,
and not by those who merely
talk about them.

James Oliver

It is work, work that one delights in, that is
the surest guarantor of happiness.
But even here it is a work that has to be
earned by labor in one's earlier years.
One should labor so hard in youth that
everything one does subsequently
is easy by comparison.

Ashley Montagu

Diligence makes good luck.

Ben Franklin

The more I want to get something done,
the less I call it work.

Richard Bach

There is no shame in asking for help.

William Glasser, M.D.

The only way to teach them to write correctly
is to have them write. A good rule would be
to have pupils write a little essay once a week.

Fanny Jackson Coppin

Life is easier when parents deliberately ignore
the daily details of their child's homework.
School assignments are the responsibility
of the child. As one father said to his son,
"Homework is for you what work is for me—
a personal responsibility."

Haim Ginott

We teachers can only help the work going on,
as servants wait upon a master.

Maria Montessori

The Value of Hard Work

One of the most important lessons that any student can learn is the value of hard work. It takes lots of effort to earn a degree, and it takes even more effort to become a success in postgraduate life. Colin Powell advised, "There are no secrets to success: Don't waste time looking for them. Success is the result of perfection, hard work, learning from failure, loyalty to those for whom you work, and persistence." General Powell was correct. There is no secret shortcut to success, but there is one surefire path that leads inexorably to the top: hard work. And, students who learn to do their best soon discover that a little extra effort can make a world of difference.

The notion that work is a burden is a terrible mistake. Working and facing up to one's responsibilities: That's happiness.

—Katharine Hepburn—

9

Order
in the Classroom

Education is teaching
children to behave
as they prefer
not to behave.

—Anonymous—

The noted writer E. B. White once observed, "If you make the work interesting, the discipline will take care of itself." Obviously, Mr. White never taught junior high. If classroom discipline were solely dependent upon subject matter, teachers everywhere could quiet their students with a few verses from Shakespeare. Unfortunately, it's not that easy.

A more realistic assessment of schoolhouse comportment was offered by Haim Ginott, who wrote, "Every teacher knows that 'Love is not enough.' Neither is 'Creating rapport' or 'Making it interesting.' Friendly adjectives do not a classroom problem solve."

The ideas contained in this chapter will not resolve all classroom difficulties, but they will help. And, if all else fails, try Shakespeare.

Life is tons of discipline.

Robert Frost

The inner landscape of many children is full of
mines ready to explode upon careless contact.
Any insulting remark can set off an explosion.

Haim Ginott

Whenever a pupil has spoken disrespectfully
to a teacher and the teacher can say with truth,
"Do I not always speak politely to you?"
the case is won without any more argument.

Fanny Jackson Coppin

In discipline, whatever generates hate
must be avoided. Whatever creates
self-esteem is to be fostered.

Haim Ginott

Good discipline is a series of little victories
in which a teacher, through small decencies,
reaches a child's heart.

Haim Ginott

Your job is to teach students that their behavior
is not caused by what happened to them,
but by what goes on inside their heads; and that
whatever they do, they are choosing to do it.

William Glasser, M.D.

I can think of no agency in the formation of a
beautiful character that is more powerful
than the daily correction and
training which we call discipline,
and here the teacher is all-powerful.

Fanny Jackson Coppin

Disciplinary problems become opportunities
for conveying values, providing insights,
and strengthening self-esteem.

Haim Ginott

Discipline is not a nasty word.

Pat Riley

When a child feels he does not deserve praise,
he may misbehave to set the adult straight.

Haim Ginott

Discipline, like surgery, requires precision—
no random cuts, no rambling comments.
Above all, a teacher demonstrates
self-discipline and good manners.

Haim Ginott

Living up to basic ethical standards in the
classroom—discipline, tolerance, honesty—
is one of the most important ways children learn
how to function in society at large.

Eloise Salholz

Talking in classes disturbs the teacher and
the class. The habit of self-control is not
easily acquired, but when the pupil has
his tongue under control, as St. James says,
"He is able also to bridle the whole body."

Fanny Jackson Coppin

Calming down a noisy, rebellious group
of adolescents is a lot like defusing a bomb.
Careful, premeditated, calm responses
are crucial to success.

James Nehring

Self-control is the highest form of rulership.

Anonymous

Self-control is the hardest victory.

Aristotle

The man who masters his own soul will forever
be called conqueror of conquerors.

Plautus

Punishments that do not correct, harden.

Fanny Jackson Coppin

Every misbehaving child is discouraged
and needs continuous encouragement,
just as a plant needs water and sunshine.

Rudolf Dreikurs

Teaching with Patience

Teaching requires patience. Even the most mannerly students do things that disappoint us, or worry us, or confuse us, or anger us from time to time. Why? Because they are not yet adults and because they are human. It is precisely *because* they are human that we must, from time to time, be patient with our students' shortcomings (just as they must, on occasion, be patient with ours). Sometimes, patience is the price we pay for being responsible teachers, and that's as it should be. After all, think how patient *our* teachers have been with us.

Speak when you're angry and you'll make the best speech you'll ever regret.

—Laurence Peter—

10

Lessons About Life

Life is a series
of lessons that
must be lived
to be understood.

—Ralph Waldo Emerson—

W. E. B. Du Bois once observed, "Education must not simply teach work, it must teach life." In this chapter, we consider a few of the most important lessons about the human condition.

Henry James advised, "Live all you can; it's a mistake not to. It doesn't so much matter what you do, so long as you have your life. If you haven't had that, what have you had?"

Thoughtful teachers help their students understand that life should be savored, not squandered. It was Bishop Fulton J. Sheen who observed, "Time is so precious that God deals it out only second by second." This earthly life is, indeed, a brief interval between birth and death. Our challenge, of course, it to determine how best to use it...and to teach our children to do the same.

May everything I see teach and
instruct me something.

Margaret Godolphin

Education is life, not books.

African Proverb

Life is painting a picture, not doing a sum.

Oliver Wendell Holmes, Jr.

Be yourself and think for yourself; and,
while your conclusions may not be infallible,
they will be nearer right than
the conclusions forced upon you.

Elbert Hubbard

Great minds have purposes;
        others have wishes.

Washington Irving

Believe that your life is worth living,
        and your belief will help create the fact.

William James

Every man's life is a plan of God.

Horace Bushnell

Every man is the architect of his own fortune.

Sallust

Life is the sum of all your choices.

Albert Camus

A human life is like a single letter in the
alphabet. It can be meaningless.
Or it can be part of a great meaning.

Jewish Theological Seminary of America

When it comes to life, the critical thing
is whether you take things for granted
or take them with gratitude.

G. K. Chesterton

Life is a great bundle of little things.

Oliver Wendell Holmes, Sr.

Life is a succession of moments;
to live each one is to succeed.

Corita Kent

Opportunity is missed by most people
because it is dressed in overalls
and looks like work.

Thomas Alva Edison

Life is always at some turning point.

Irwin Edman

All life is an experiment.
The more experiments you make, the better.

Ralph Waldo Emerson

There is no security on this earth;
there is only opportunity.

Douglas MacArthur

For when the one Great Scorer comes
to write against your name, He marks
not that you won or lost, but
how you played the game.

Grantland Rice

When fate hands you a lemon,
make lemonade.

Dale Carnegie

What education I have received has been
gained in the University of Life.

Horatio Bottomley

To improve the golden moment of opportunity
and catch the good that is within our reach
is the great art of life.

Samuel Johnson

Celebrating Today

When we begin to search for reason's to celebrate the gift of life, we find them all around us. Each new dawn breaks upon a day filled with countless possibilities. To forget to say "thank you" for these gifts is not simply poor manners, it is also sloppy thinking. Wise teachers give thanks for this opportunity called life, and they teach their students to do likewise.

Write on your heart
that every day is the
best day of the year.

—Ralph Waldo Emerson—

11

The School of
Hard Knocks

Good people are good because they've come to wisdom through failure.

—William Saroyan—

Frederick Phillips noted, "It is often hard to distinguish between the hard knocks in life and those of opportunity." Anyone who has been knocked down by life will attest that these opportunities are not only hard to see but are sometimes almost invisible.

American poet Ella Wheeler Wilcox wrote, "From the discontent of man, the world's best progress springs." In this chapter we consider the entrance requirements, the curriculum, and the honored graduates of a school that has changed the world like no other: the school of hard knocks.

Times of general calamity and confusion
have ever been productive of the greatest minds.
The purest ore is produced from the hottest
furnace, and the brightest thunderbolt is
elicited from the darkest storms.

Charles Caleb Colton

Problems are the cutting edge that
distinguishes between success and failure.
Problems create our courage and wisdom.

M. Scott Peck

Obstacles cannot crush me; every obstacle
yields to stern resolve.

Leonardo da Vinci

God helps those who persevere.

The Koran

Do you desire to know the art of living
my friend? It is contained in one phrase:
Make use of suffering.

Henri Frédéric Amiel

A diamond is a chunk of coal
that made good under pressure.

Anonymous

People seldom see the halting and
painful steps by which the most
insignificant success is achieved.

Annie Sullivan

Character cannot be developed in ease
and quiet. Only through the experience
of trial and suffering can the soul
be strengthened, vision cleared,
ambition inspired, and success achieved.

Helen Keller

A problem is a chance for you to do your best.

Duke Ellington

The game of life is not so much in holding
a good hand as playing a poor hand well.

H. T. Leslie

No pain, no palm; no thorns, no throne;
no gall, no glory; no cross, no crown.

William Penn

The way I see it, if you want the rainbow,
you've got to put up with the rain.

Dolly Parton

Adversity causes some men to break,
others to break records.

William A. Ward

The difficulties and struggles of today are but the price we must pay for the accomplishments and victories of tomorrow.

William J. H. Boetcker

Real miracles are created by men when they use their God-given courage and intelligence.

Jean Anouilh

Things turn out best for people who make the best of the way things turn out.

Anonymous

Poverty must not be a bar to learning, and learning must offer an escape from poverty.

Lyndon B. Johnson

With luck and resolution and good guidance, the human mind can survive not only poverty—but even wealth.

Gilbert Highet

Although there are countless alumni of the school of hard knocks, there has not yet been a move to accredit that institution.

—Sonya Rudikoff—

Difficulties are meant to rouse, not discourage.
The human spirit grows strong by conflict.

William Ellery Channing

It is not in the still calm of life, or
in repose of pacific station that
great characters are formed....
Great necessities call out great virtues.

Abigail Adams

He that wrestles with us strengthens our
nerves and sharpens our skills.
Our antagonist is our helper.

Edmund Burke

The block of granite which was an obstacle
in the path of the weak becomes
a stepping-stone in the path of the strong.

Thomas Carlyle

Adversity introduces a man to himself.

Anonymous

Our trials are tests; our sorrows pave the
way for a fuller life when we have earned it.

Jerome P. Fleishman

I walk firmer and more secure up hill than down.

Michel de Montaigne

The gem cannot be polished without friction
nor man perfected without trials.

Confucius

Learning at the School of Hard Knocks

A hundred years before the birth of Christ, Publilius Syrus observed, "Many receive advice, few profit from it." For twenty-one centuries, teachers everywhere have known exactly how he felt.

In a 1955 television interview, Harry Truman commented, "I have always found the best way to give advice to your children is to find out what they want and then advise them to do it." Obviously, President Truman spoke from experience. No matter how sound a parent or teacher's recommendations may be, some children seem destined to learn life's lessons the hard way.

The school of hard knocks is a difficult place to matriculate, but its doors are always open and children are always willing to attend. As caring teachers, we can lecture, cajole, and plead with our students. But sometimes, all we can do is wait for them to grow up...and pray that they will graduate from the school of hard knocks sooner rather than later.

Not the school,
nor the teachers,
but the student is the
preponderant factor
in education.

—James Weldon Johnson—

12

Lessons Beyond
the Classroom

It is no profit to have learned well if you neglect to do well.

—Publilius Syrus—

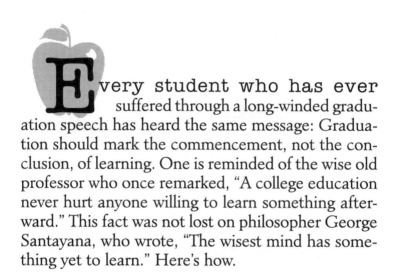

Every student who has ever suffered through a long-winded graduation speech has heard the same message: Graduation should mark the commencement, not the conclusion, of learning. One is reminded of the wise old professor who once remarked, "A college education never hurt anyone willing to learn something afterward." This fact was not lost on philosopher George Santayana, who wrote, "The wisest mind has something yet to learn." Here's how.

They go forth with well-developed bodies,
fairly developed minds, and undeveloped hearts.
An undeveloped heart—not a cold one.
The difference is important.

E. M. Forster

The fireworks begin today.
Each diploma is a lighted match.
Each one of you is a fuse.

Edward Koch

I ask you to decide, as Goethe put it,
whether you will be an anvil or a hammer.
The question is whether you are to be a hammer—
whether you are to give to the world in which
you were reared and educated the broadest
possible benefits of that education.

John F. Kennedy

Life is a glorious opportunity.

Billy Graham

The secret of joy in work is contained in one word—excellence. To know how to do something well is to enjoy it.

Pearl Buck

Always aim for achievement, and forget about success.

Helen Hayes

When it becomes necessary to do a thing, the whole heart and soul should go into the measure, or not attempt it.

Thomas Paine

Nothing is really work unless you would rather be doing something else.

Sir James M. Barrie

The work of the individual still remains
the spark that moves mankind ahead,
even more than teamwork.

Igor Sikorsky

I long to accomplish a great and noble task,
but it is my chief duty to accomplish humble
tasks as though they were great and noble.
The world is moved along, not only by the mighty
shoves of its heroes but also by the aggregate
of the tiny pushes of each honest worker.

Helen Keller

The most instructive experiences
are those of everyday life.

Friedrich Nietzsche

Like what you do. If you don't like it,
do something else.

Paul Harvey

Observations more than books, experiences
rather than persons are the prime educators.

Bronson Alcott

Instruction ends in the schoolroom,
but education ends only with life.

F. W. Robertson

It is always in season for old men to learn.

Aeschylus

The brighter you are, the more you have to learn.

Don Herold

The essence of knowledge is, having it, to use it.

Confucius

Anyone who stops learning is old,
whether at twenty or eighty.

Henry Ford

A man, though wise, should never be
ashamed of learning more.

Sophocles

A man should never stop learning,
even on his last day.

Maimonides

One's work may be finished some day,
but one's education, never.

Alexandre Dumas

When you're green, you're growing;
when you're ripe, you rot.

Ray Kroc

Teaching Life

The ultimate goal of education is, of course, preparation for life. Thus, the greatest teachers are those who teach—by their words and their examples—the art of living.

Teachers change the world by changing their students. Successful teachers help their students celebrate the gift of life and use that gift to the fullest extent possible. When they do, the students' lives are changed forever...and so is the world.

As long as you live, keep learning how to live.

—Seneca—

13

Observations About Learning

It is impossible for a man to learn
    that which he thinks he already knows.

                                   Epictetus

The doer alone learneth.

                        Friedrich Nietzsche

Listen rather than lecture. Show the road
    but expect the child to reach
    his destination on his own.

                             Haim Ginott

Use fewer examinations, fewer quizzes,
    and more essay assignments. You don't know
anything about a subject until you can put your
    knowledge into some kind of expression.

                          Wayne C. Booth

We teach who we are.

                           John Gardner

Stay interested in everything and everybody.
It keeps you young.

Marie T. Freeman

Good manners will often take people where
neither money nor education will take them.

Fanny Jackson Coppin

Wisdom is oftentimes nearer when we stoop
than when we soar.

William Wordsworth

What we have to learn to do, we learn by doing.

Aristotle

My definition of an educated man is the
fellow who knows the right thing to do
at the time it has to be done.

Charles F. Kettering

We live in a time of such rapid change
and growth of knowledge that only he who
is in a fundamental sense a scholar—that is,
a person who continues to learn and inquire—
can hope to keep pace, let alone play
the role of guide.

Nathan M. Pusey

The problem is not to suppress change,
which cannot be done, but to manage it.

Alvin Toffler

Only in growth, reform, and change,
paradoxically enough, is true security found.

Anne Morrow Lindbergh

Education consists mainly
in what we have unlearned.

Mark Twain

The spiritual seeker says, "My life is a classroom.
I am learning something important,
even from this."

Mary Hayes-Grieco

Unholy ambition never succeeds well in
anything, nor will the Great Creator reveal
His secrets to those whose only desire is
to shine in the eyes of men. But the light of
Heaven will shine all around the man who humbly
and fervently asks for more light, more light.

Fanny Jackson Coppin

I learn from anyone, but I do not stop at that.
I go on trying to learn from myself.

Zane Grey

It's what you learn after you know it all
that counts.

Harry S. Truman

The art of being wise is knowing what to overlook.

William James

Life is a festival only to the wise.

Ralph Waldo Emerson

I am still learning.

Michelangelo's Favorite Saying

I am not young enough to know everything.

Sir James M. Barrie

The excitement of learning separates
youth from old age.
As long as you're learning you're not old.

Rosalyn Sussman Yalow

I touch the future.
I teach.

—Christa McAuilffe—

About the Author

Criswell Freeman is a Doctor of Clinical Psychology living in Nashville, Tennessee. He is the author of *When Life Throws You a Curveball, Hit It* and numerous books in the Forever Series published by WALNUT GROVE PRESS.

Dr. Freeman's Wisdom Books chronicle memorable quotations in an easy-to-read style. The series provides inspiring, thoughtful and humorous messages from entertainers, athletes, scientists, politicians, clerics, writers and renegades, with each title focusing on a particular region or area of special interest. Combining his passion for quotations with extensive training in psychology, Freeman revisits timeless themes such as perseverance, courage, love, forgiveness and faith.

Dr. Freeman is also the host of *Wisdom Made in America*, a nationally syndicated radio program.